Polar Bears Live on Ice

Melvin and Gilda Berger

SCHOLASTIC INC.
New York Toronto London Auckland Sydney
Mexico City New Delhi Hong Kong Buenos Aires

Photographs: Cover: Tui De Roy/Bruce Coleman, Inc., New York; p. 1: E. R. Degginger/Bruce Coleman, Inc.; p. 3: E. R. Degginger/Bruce Coleman, Inc.; p. 4: Tui De Roy/Bruce Coleman, Inc.; p. 5: Hans Reinhard/Bruce Coleman, Inc.; p. 6: Stephen J. Krasemann/Photo Researchers, New York; p. 7: Mark J. Thomas/Dembinsky Photo Associates, Owosso, MI; p. 8: John Swedberg/Bruce Coleman, Inc.; p. 9: Dan Guravich/Photo Researchers; 10: Tom Brakefield/Bruce Coleman, Inc.; p. 11: Fritz Polking/Bruce Coleman, Inc.; p. 12: Norbert Rosing/Animals Animals, Chatham, NY; p. 13: In The Light/Peter Arnold Inc., New York; p. 14: Dan Guravich/Photo Researchers; p. 15: Dan Guravich/Photo Researchers; p. 16: Steven Kazlowski/Peter Arnold, Inc.

Book design by Annette Cyr

ISBN 0-439-47181-8

12 11 10 9 8 7   5 6 7 8/0

Printed in the U.S.A.
First printing, January 2003

Polar bears live on ice.

The ice is on top of the water.

Fun Fact

Hair on the bottoms of polar bears' paws helps to keep their paws warm.

The ice is on top of the land.

Fun Fact

Polar bears have big, flat paws. The bears walk on the snow without falling in.

Polar bears live on snow.

Polar bears rest on snow.

Polar bears have thick coats
of fur to keep them warm.

Polar bears are hard
to see in the snow.

Fun Fact

Female polar bears dig their dens in snow, ice, or in the ground.

Female polar bears build dens.

Female bears sleep in
their dens all winter.

Fun Fact

Female polar bears usually give birth to two cubs while half asleep.

Polar bear cubs are born in the den.

The mother polar bear
feeds her cubs.

Fun Fact

At first, cubs only spend a short time outside the den before going back in.

In spring, the polar bears come out of the den.

The mother polar bear teaches her cubs to swim.

The mother polar bear teaches
her cubs to live on ice.